Many people think Christianity is not for the likes of them. But what if God exists? That would change everything. God - Is He out There? is a clear explanation of what God says about himself without talking down to people. It's a great opportunity to think about the most important questions of all: Does God exist? What's he like? And what's it got to do with me?

Tim Chester
Pastor with Grace Church, Boroughbridge,
tutor with the Acts 29 Oak Hill Academy and author of over 30 books

I would be the last person to say we need another evangelistic tool in the midst of so many already. That is, until I read this first workbook, God - Is He Out There?, by Mez McConnell. It is brilliantly simple and accessible to anyone searching for answers about God and truth, and yet biblically sound and clear about what it truly means to know Christ and walk with him. Mez has a sensitive pastor's heart and a burdened for the urban poor that oozes with every page. This book is a clear and needed contribution from one of the most careful and wise thinkers on caring for the poor in our generation.

Brian Croft
Senior Pastor, Auburndale Baptist Church, Louisville, Kentucky,
Senior Fellow, Church Revitalization Center,
The Southern Baptist Theological Seminary , Louisville, Kentucky

A bangin' little book for those asking life's big questions...especially those who don't know about Jesus!

Dai Hankey
Cheeky git and gospel ninja!
(... and Pastor of Hill City Church, Pontnewynydd, Wales)

A life committed to following Jesus isn't easy, so we need all the help we can get! I'm thankful, then, for a resource like this. In God - Is He Out There?, Mez McConnell tackles the difficult — yet central — questions of Christian theology in a way that is accessible, practical, and personal.

Jared Wilson
Director of Content Strategy, Midwestern Baptist Theological Seminary,
Kansas City, Missouri and M
Midwestern's

God – Is He Out There? is such a practical tool for discipling believers in the basics of the Christian faith. Both new and mature Christians will find Mez's book helpful for understanding some of the foundational questions most of us have. My advice: Grab a copy and walk with a few others believers through it.

Robby Gallaty
Senior Pastor, Long Hollow Baptist Church,
Hendersonville, Tennessee

Mez McConnell gives us a beautiful and relatable road map to walking someone through the most important questions they'll ever have. God-Is he out there, connects the dots between our doubts and the divine. A wonderful read.

Albert Tate
Founder & lead pastor, Fellowship Monrovia, Monrovia, California and contributor to *Letters to a Birmingham Jail: A Response to the Words and Dreams of Dr. Martin Luther King Jr.*

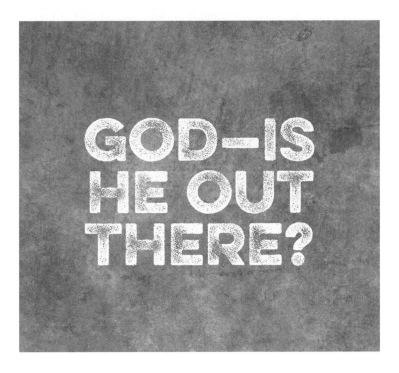

Mez McConnell

CHRISTIAN FOCUS

IX **9Marks** Urban

IX 9Marks Urban

This series of short workbooks, from the 9Marks Urban series, are designed to help you think through some of life's big questions.

Copyright © Mez McConnell 2016

paperback ISBN 978-1-78191-710-7
epub ISBN 978-1-78191-791-6
mobi ISBN 978-1-78191-792-3

10 9 8 7 6 5 4 3 2 1

Published in 2016
by
Christian Focus Publications Ltd,
Geanies House, Fearn, Ross-shire,
IV20 1TW, Great Britain.

www.christianfocus.com

Cover and Interior Design by
Moose77.com

Printed and bound
by
Bell & Bain, Glasgow

CONTENTS

INTRODUCTION

Life is full of questions. Now some questions are really not all that important, like what should I wear today or are we going out tonight. Then there are the big questions, the kind of questions that might keep you up at night. Will she ever forgive me? How am I going to get money to pay off that debt? How am I going to get out of this mess?

What about the really big questions, the questions that define us, questions that help us make sense of the world we are living in? Is there really a God? If there is a God, why is life so difficult? What is the point of my life? What happens when I die?

This series of short workbooks are designed to help you think through some of life's big questions. It all starts with the most important question of all: **God—Is He Out There?** The questions that follow all hinge on our answer to that question. If we answer that there is a God, then how can we get to know Him and how should we now live?

In this book we will meet Jack. Jack is an ordinary man in many ways. He will probably remind you of someone you already know. Perhaps he will remind you of yourself. Jack has come to the point in his life when he has started asking some really serious questions and he is desperate for answers. Throughout this series of books we will be walking with Jack as he discovers those answers. More than likely, the questions that Jack is asking are some of the same questions you have been wondering about. So throughout this workbook, and the ones that follow, seek to discover some big answers to these big questions.

To get the most out of this series of books read a chapter and then discuss it with a Christian. Perhaps you are curious about Christianity, or maybe you yourself are a new Christian seeking to discover some of the basics about your new relationship with Jesus. Either way my prayer is that you will find these books to be a helpful tool as you seek to discover answers to life's big questions.

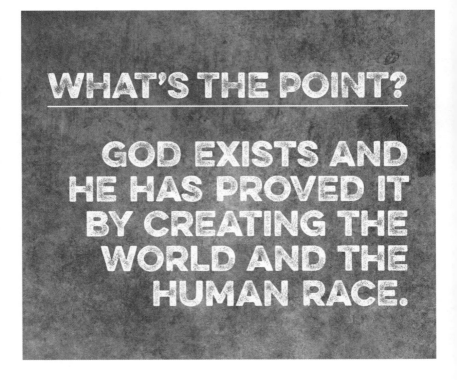

WHAT'S THE POINT?

GOD EXISTS AND HE HAS PROVED IT BY CREATING THE WORLD AND THE HUMAN RACE.

IF GOD EXISTS, PROVE IT THEN!

(PART 1)

JACK'S STORY

Jack shuffles into the church building one day looking a little unsteady on his feet. A big, powerfully built man, he mumbles something about God and the church and slumps into a chair. After a bit of coercion you discover that he is in his mid-30s and comes from a Catholic background. The slurring, he claims, is down to his prescribed medication but you suspect that he is more than a little high on some form of street drug.

It turns out that he has heard about the church from friends and wants help to get his life sorted, even though he has no idea what he means by that. With a little questioning you discover that he is religious in that he believes in a God of some sort. He just doesn't know what. In Jack's mind, if there is a God, then He is definitely not interested in people like him. Jack has no clue about the Bible and he thinks the church is just for old women and posh people. But he's turned up because he's desperate to turn things around and this is the last resort.

Recently, his life has begun to seriously decline. One of his closest friends died of an overdose and he feels like his heroin habit is spiralling out of control. He's beginning to wonder more about the point of life. Why are we here? What's it all about? Is there any meaning to it all? He's full of doubt, fear, anger and questions.

WHERE DO WE BEGIN WITH JACK?

Jack asks some great questions.

> Why are we here?
> What are we doing on this big globe we call earth?
> What is the point of it all?

These are the big questions of our day. Indeed they are the big questions of the history of the human race. We all want to find meaning in our lives — whether we come to church and believe in God or not. We want our lives to mean something. We want to think there is some significance to it all.

> Who are we really?
> What are we all about?

One thing is for certain. Most of us, like Jack, would be pretty confident that the Bible and the church have got nothing much to offer when it comes to this stuff.

But Jack, like most people, would be wrong.

ILLUSTRATION

I play a game with my two girls every year on their birthday and at Christmas. Like all children, they absolutely adore receiving and opening presents. They are just desperate to know what presents my wife and I have bought them and they will try any and every trick to find out ahead of time what's inside the packaging. Without fail one of them will sidle up to me at some point and ask what I have bought for the other one with the promise that, 'I will keep the secret. You can trust me, dad. I won't say anything.' I always refuse, tell them to wait and they squeal with frustration. They want to know. They *need* to know. Instead, I keep my mouth shut until the day arrives and they can find out for themselves what the gift is. But that doesn't stop them trying other tactics. So, if they can't get me to tell them then they begin trying to guess. They shake the box and shout out hundreds of different things hoping to pick up a clue in my reactions. Sometimes they convince themselves it is a particular thing right up to the moment they open the present and discover something different altogether. The only way they ever have real certainty about what is inside the wrapping paper is to tear it off and reveal what's underneath. That's when they finally know for sure what their gift is. Almost always it is never what they thought it was going to be and they are usually miles off the mark.

The same can be said about discovering the truth about God.

Many people think they know the answers to the secrets of the universe. Many people like to make wild guesses. They come up with all sorts of weird and wonderful ideas about how the human race came into existence. Does the Vatican sit on top of a giant spacecraft? Are we descended from an alien life force? Are we nothing more than evolved beasts?

Who knows?
Can we ever know for sure anyway?

Jack is one of those guys that think nobody can know for certain if God exists and nobody could ever know for sure what He is like. In Jack's world God is

unprovable
and
unknowable.

STOP

Q: What do we think? Is Jack right? Can the existence of God be proved? Can anybody really claim to know God for sure?

🚀 ILLUSTRATION

Imagine if we had to spend our entire lives sitting in a room without any windows. There is a door in this room but the handle is on the other side. In other words, there is no way out and there is no way of knowing what is on the other side of that door. There may be something and there may be nothing. You and your friends are constantly trying to figure the problem out. Some of them claim to hear noises out there but others say it's all in their imaginations. Some people try and guess what's out there and some can't be bothered because, after all, most of it is pure speculation. Some people are claiming they know 100% what is out there even though they've never ventured out of the room in their life. The bottom line is that none of the people in the room know for sure.

That is how most people think of the meaning of life and the existence of God.

The human race is trapped on this planet and many believe that we have no way of knowing for sure if there is anything out there. So, anybody who claims to know for sure is met with suspicion. How can we know anything for sure? Have we seen it with our own eyes? Where is the proof? The only way anybody in that room could have certainty about what was on the other side of the door is if it was opened and revealed to them.

This is always the first lesson a person has to accept about the Christian faith. This is what Jack has to understand.

We can never know anything for certain about the existence of God unless HE chooses to reveal it to us.

Google can't help us.
Our friends can't help us.

The only way anybody can know for sure is if the God *'out there'* reveals Himself to us *'down here'*. This is precisely what the Christian faith claims He has done.

1. GOD HAS REVEALED HIMSELF IN THE WORLD HE HAS MADE.

What does Jack believe about the world that he sees? He's not sure. Evolution, right? That's a (sort of) fact in Jack's mind. Yet, he doesn't quite know how to explain it. He just takes it as a fact because that's what scientists say and, anyway, he saw a bit of a programme on the TV about it once. Also, there was a Big Bang, wasn't there? He doesn't actually think about it much because it gives him a bit of a headache. Again, he doesn't really know how the world got here but it can't be God because nobody really believes that stuff anymore, do they? For Jack life is almost completely pointless. We live and die and that's it. There might be a God and there might not. Who knows? Who cares? What does it matter? It's not going to make his life better one bit, is it?

STOP

Q: What do we think about Jack's view of the world? How do we think the world got here? Does it matter? If so, why? If not, why not?

The Bible has a different view of the world than Jack's. In fact the Bible says that one of the ways God has revealed Himself to us is:

through this world that He has made.

'The heavens declare the glory of God, and the sky above proclaims his handiwork.' (Psalm 19:1)

'For what can be known about God is plain to them [the human race], because God has shown it to them. For his invisible attributes, namely, his eternal power and divine nature, have been clearly perceived, ever since the creation of the world, in the things that have been made. So they [the human race] are without excuse.' (Romans 1:19-20)

ILLUSTRATION

If we opened up the bonnet of a car and found a brand new engine we wouldn't, for one second, think that it got there by itself. Each part of the machine has a part to play in making the whole thing run smoothly. A working engine is a feat of creative and engineering genius. God proves His existence to the human race by His creation of the world, which is a work of stunning genius from start to finish.

JACK

'Hang on a minute,' says Jack. 'If that's true then why is this world so messed up? Why so much pain and suffering?'

Good questions.
We will get to them later in our studies on God.

But right now we are trying to lay the foundations. Once we get the foundations in we can start looking at some of the problem areas. For now, back to the point:

God has chosen to reveal Himself to the world through the creation He has made.

> **STOP**
> Q: *What sort of things can we know about God just by looking at the world?*

He must be **smart** when you think about how all things hold together in this world.

He must be **creative** when you think about the beauty and variety of created things.

He must be **powerful** when you think about the mountains, the seas and the powerful forces at work in our universe.

What's even more incredible is that God did all this simply by speaking it into existence. Many people want to write off the world as a cosmic accident, a chance event or the result of a bang. But the world around us speaks of a great designer, a planner, somebody creative and, above all, somebody extremely powerful.

2. GOD HAS REVEALED HIMSELF IN THE CREATION OF THE HUMAN RACE.

The world is an amazing place full of many wonders but there is nothing on the planet to compare to the human race. But let's remember that Jack believes in evolution and, therefore, doesn't think that human beings are any more important or different than any other creature on earth. Or does he?

> **STOP**
>
> Q: *Is there a difference between a human baby and a puppy? Is one of them more valuable than the other? Defend your answers.*

Human beings are extremely complex creations. Even something as small as the human eyeball is just so intricate and well put together. The retina contains 130 million rod shaped cells, which transmit impulses to the brain through 1 million fibres, and handles 0.5 million messages simultaneously. It is a feat of design and engineering. We could go through practically every other organ in the body and discover similar marvels.

> **JACK**
>
> *'So what!' says Jack. 'Dogs have eyes. Don't we share the same DNA with apes too?'* So that proves the Bible is wrong!

> **STOP**
>
> *Do we agree with Jack? What, if anything, makes us different from the animal world?*

WE ARE INTIMATELY FORMED

Genesis teaches us that. God is clearly active in the creation of the world and all living things, including us. Look at the language of Genesis 2:7.

Man was 'formed' by God and then <u>He breathed life into us.</u>

That suggests intimacy and craft—there is no room for an evolutionary process at this point. We were formed from the earth and we return to the earth. Our very breath here is a God-given gift – there is intimacy in our creation. He didn't just start a process and stand back from it to let it develop.

WE ARE MADE IN HIS IMAGE

God said, *'Let us make mankind in our image and according to our likeness'* (Genesis 1:26). There are obviously similarities between man and the animals. Both were created from the same matter (dust), both given the breath of life and, therefore, many see a close link between humanity and the animal kingdom. But, in so many ways, we stand apart from the animal kingdom. We are similar yet, Genesis teaches, we are so very different. We are created in the image of God and animals are not.

The root of the Hebrew word for image, **tselem**, appears to mean 'to carve', or 'cut up'. In other words, man is almost literally a chip off the old block. But what does it mean? Are we literally little gods then, as Mormons would have us believe? No, not really. Does God have a physical body then? No, He is a spirit, the Bible teaches us.

But man does have
> **reason,**
> **intellect,**
> **will,**
> **morality,**
> **a conscience**
> **and emotion**

and in Adam we were created
> **sinless**
> **and good.**

We have
> **the ability to communicate in languages,**
> **creativity,**
> **love,**
> **holiness,**
> **immortality**
> **and**
> **freedom.**

It is important that we understand the high nature of our creation and that is why the Bible mentions the phrase 'image of God' three times in two verses (Genesis 1:26-27). It is clear that both men and women share a common humanity and an equal worth before God, but it is interesting that they are not equal in terms of being constituted in His image in exactly the same way. Man is from dust and woman is from his flesh and bones. Woman is dependent on the man. Yet man is also dependent on the woman, 'for as woman was made from man, so man is now born of woman. And all things are from God' (1 Corinthians 11:12).

**Men and women are worthy of equal dignity —
only evolution reduces us to the same worth as a flea.**

Man and woman are the crowning glory of God's creation. And all of this is described in the Bible as 'very good.'

The work of creating humanity is finished.

In other words, the human race was made
**for God
and
by God.**

HUMAN BEINGS HAVE SOULS

It is the soul that gives us a unique place in the world. It is what connects us to God. It's what makes us know deep down inside that there is something more to life than what we currently experience. (It is one of the reasons that Jack feels as empty as he does.) The human race has been made with an ability to question and a deep sense of right and wrong. When we lie to people, whether we are Christians or not, we know deep inside it's wrong. When we hurt another person, we know deep inside it's wrong. We know, through our conscience, when we have done a wrong thing.

**Nobody has to tell us this.
We just know.
Where does this come from?**

The Bible says in Romans 2:14-15 that we know right and wrong because God has written His law on our hearts. He has engraved it there, even before we were born. Every human being is born with a conscience. It tells us that the person who created us is righteous and holy and perfect and good. God put these things into our hearts so that when we do wrong we would not have any excuse.

 MEMORY VERSE
'The heavens declare the glory of God, and the sky above proclaims his handiwork.' (Psalm 19:1)

 SUMMARY
Jack needs to know that life is not pointless. It is not random. God does exist and God does care about him and his life. The world around us, and even Jack himself, is proof of God's existence.

But there's more...

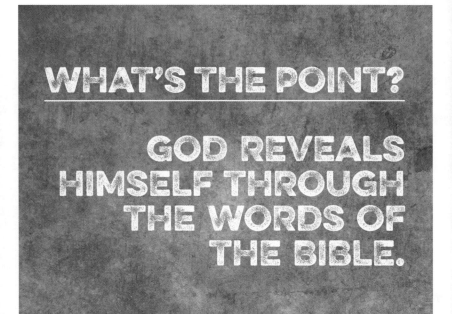

WHAT'S THE POINT?

GOD REVEALS HIMSELF THROUGH THE WORDS OF THE BIBLE.

IF GOD EXISTS, PROVE IT THEN!
(PART II)

RECAP

God has proven Himself by:

1. *Creating the world*
2. *Creating the human race.*

Q: What do these things teach us about what God is like?

He is powerful,
   creative
      and good.

But God has also revealed Himself in another way to us.

He has spoken.
The Christian God is a talking God. He speaks to us through the pages of the Bible.

JACK

Like most people Jack hasn't got the first clue about the Bible. He's sure there's one in his Nan's house but he's never had much to do with it. He may have read the odd bit of it here and there but mostly the only thing he knows about it is what he and his friends have found online from conspiracy theorists. As far as he is concerned, the Bible is old-fashioned, full of mistakes and out of date. It may have been good in his Nan's day but it is irrelevant for him and his life. Anyway, according to Jack, science has disproved most of it and it's hard to believe fairy stories like people living in giant fish and stuff like that. In his mind, you'd have to be mad to live your life according to the Bible.

STOP

Q: What do you think of Jack's view of the Bible? Do you agree or disagree? Why?

What if we were to throw our Bibles in the bin? Would the world around us give us enough information to find out what God is truly like? As we've discovered, creation tells us *some things* about God but it doesn't tell us *everything* about Him. The existence of trees might tell us that there's something out there that is quite creative but it doesn't tell us anything specific about our purpose in the world, does it?

In fact, there's only one place in the universe where we can find out true and specific facts about what God requires from the human race.

The Bible.
It is there that we discover
  Who He is,
    what He is like,
      who we are and
        what He expects from us.

For these reasons it is vitally important to the life of the Christian.

We need the Bible because:
1. It tells us what we are like as a human race
2. It tells us what God is like
3. It tells us how each of us can come to know God personally.

What do we do these days if we want to know the quick answer to something? Well we probably get out our smartphones to Google it. Or, if we're really old school, we might ask somebody that we know. Now the problem is, particularly on the internet, that there are a lot of fruitcakes and conspiracy theorists out there. There are all sorts of weird and wacky people in the world with all sorts of crackpot ideas, particularly when it comes to the Bible.

How do we know what's reliable and what's not?
How do we know that we're not being given dodgy information?

 ## ILLUSTRATION

If we have a problem with our car, for instance, it's no good looking up a microwave manual. That's not going to help us. We need to take the car to a garage and find a mechanic who knows what he's talking about.

So when we want to find out about the gospel, we don't need to go to some illuminati website or go and see our uncle Bob who went to church once a while ago.

We need to go to the source material.
We need to check out the original handbook.
We need to go to the Bible.

Only this book has the **authority** to tell us what the gospel really means and why it really matters.

In fact the Bible is the <u>only</u> trustworthy place that we can find out about God in our world.

STOP
Is the entire Bible true, or just some of it? Which parts are true and which are not? How do we tell the difference?

We live in a world where people think that Bible-believing Christians are idiots for taking it all so seriously. How can Christians believe some stupid old book written thousands of years ago by superstitious half-wits?

This is the new millennium. We've moved on, haven't we?
Surely no intelligent person believes all that mumbo jumbo in the Bible, do they?

That's what Jack and his friends and family think about these issues. According to Jack's friends, that's what most normal people (those in their right minds anyway) think about it too. The Bible may be interesting to read in parts but that is about as far as it goes. A few good stories, maybe some decent moral advice here and there, but nothing more than that.

Bible believing Christians, on the other hand, believe and teach that not only is the Bible
100% true

it is also
100% trustworthy

and
100% God's Holy Word.

JACK
'Come on man,' he says. 'Nobody believes the Bible is 100% true. It is just stories patched together by cavemen. It's full of mistakes and contradictions. How can that be trustworthy?'

The problem is Jack says these things but he doesn't know how to back them up. How can he know that a book he has never read is so full of mistakes? When we ask him to point out the contradictions, he cannot. So, let's give him a helping hand.

In Mark 15:25 we read, *'And it was the third hour when they crucified him.'* Yet, in John 19:14 we read, *'Now it was the day of Preparation of the Passover. It was about the sixth hour. He said to the Jews, "Behold your King!"'* Mark says Christ was crucified on the third hour, yet John quite clearly states that He was still on trial on the sixth hour. So how could Jesus still be on trial in the book of John three hours after Mark claims He was supposed to have been crucified? It doesn't make sense.

It looks like a glaring error.

JACK

You show it to Jack triumphantly and ask, *'Is this the kind of mistake you mean?'* He's not quite sure how to respond to that. After all, he's supposed to be the one attacking the Bible, not you. *'Exactly,'* he says. *'If the Bible is wrong here, then it can't be trusted, can it? Agreed?'* You ask him. *'Agreed,'* he responds.

What really blows his mind is when in your next breath you inform him that, despite these verses, you are still convinced that the Bible is <u>100% error free</u>.

The word we use for this is **INERRANT**.

God has written every single word in the Bible and He never, ever makes mistakes. Now Jack is even more confused. He asks, *'How can you believe that, yet you've shown me these two verses?'*

Now, this so-called mistake is easy to defend. There is no difference in the time of the trial and crucifixion of the Lord Jesus Christ despite what the texts say. You see John was following a Roman numbering and time system, because he wrote his gospel in Ephesus, which was the Roman capital of Asia. We know this for a fact because he uses this system elsewhere in the Bible. Mark consistently uses a Hebrew numbering and timing system. The third hour according to Mark's Hebrew time system was 9 a.m. and the sixth hour according to John's Roman time system was 6 a.m. So there is no mistake. Christ was tried at 6 a.m. and crucified at 9 a.m. that same morning. This matches with the other gospel accounts.

Parts of the Bible often thought to be contradictory actually have perfectly reasonable explanations.

The Bible is a special book; in fact it is a fantastic book.

<u>How many of us think the same things as our parents or our grandparents?</u> Not many.

Do we still think the same and agree with the same things as people 100 years ago? No we don't.

Yet here we have a book that is in reality
a library of 66 books
written over a period of **1500 years**,
by over **40 different authors** from all walks of life: kings, philosophers, fishermen, poets, intellectuals.

Written in different places: in the desert, in a dungeon, in a palace, on an island, in captivity.

Written during times of war and times of peace. During times of great joy and happiness as well as times of great sorrow and grief.

Written in Asia, Africa and Europe. In Hebrew, Aramaic and Greek.

Written about hundreds of different topics.

Most of these authors never met. They never knew one another. They didn't get together down at their local coffee shop to work it all out. **Despite this, every person and every book agrees with and complements the others**.

And they all tell the story of the coming of the Lord Jesus Christ.

That makes it a special book.
A unique book.

The Bible claims to be God's own word.

3 *'All Scripture is God-breathed and is useful for teaching, rebuking, correcting and training in righteousness'* (2 Timothy 3:16, NIV).

That means God and the Bible cannot be separated. That's why we call it God's Word.
God called men from all of these places and told them what to write down.

These men are known as prophets.

> He guided them so that what they recorded is exactly what He wanted them to write.

They kept their own styles of writing and personalities (we see it in different kinds of books) but they were kept from error. These men weren't allowed to add their own thoughts and notes.

3

'No prophecy of Scripture came about by the prophet's own interpretation of things. For prophecy never had its origin in the human will, but prophets, though human, spoke from God as they were carried along by the Holy Spirit.' (2 Peter 1:20-21, NIV).

The Bible is God's message from beginning to end.

The Bible was originally written on scrolls. These original documents are called
AUTOGRAPHS.

Because papyrus was so delicate, copies had to be constantly made of the original scrolls to keep them safe. They were all done by hand. They used every safeguard to protect the accurate translation of God's Word. They didn't want to mess it up. There were no photocopiers, so they counted every letter and every word whilst they did their work. They were called scribes. How do we know they were accurate? In the 1940s the Dead Sea Scrolls were found. They contained the oldest manuscripts of the Old Testament we have. When they were compared with more recent manuscripts they found no major differences in the texts.

The Bible is
TRUSTWORTHY.

It is the most quoted, most published, most read and most influential book in the history of mankind.

3

'Your word, Lord, is eternal; it stands firm in the heavens.' (Psalm 119:89, NIV).

The Bible is God's actual, literal Word given to the human race. It is not the writings of men trying to guess what God is like but God Himself speaking through the pages of the Bible. He spoke to men and they wrote it down.

STOP
Q: Why do you think this is so important to understand?

JACK
Now Jack begins to see that the Bible is a much bigger deal than he ever realised. He thinks about the old worn-out Bible on his Nan's bookshelf and for the first time considers actually picking it up and reading it. You see Jack had all these opinions about the Bible but had never taken the time himself to read it. He asks himself, 'If the Bible can be proven to be trustworthy, then what does it actually say?'

The Bible is not just any old book. It is not an ordinary book. It is God's word breathed out through human authors.

3 *'And we also thank God continually because, when you received the word of God, which you heard from us, you accepted it not as a human word, but as it actually is, the word of God, which is indeed at work in you who believe'* (1 Thessalonians 2:13, NIV).

STOP
Q: How can we know for sure that the Bible is really God's word and not just cleverly made up stories?

The Holy Spirit did a special work when producing the Bible. People wrote down what God moved them to write.

Read 2 Peter 1:20-21 again. Do you see that it teaches God is the Bible's author?

Because the Bible is God's Word, it is useful to help us grow in understanding and righteousness. This is why we have to study it. This is why we have to be reading it.

God has given us the Bible to help us grow and become more like Jesus.

 MEMORY VERSE

'All Scripture is God-breathed and is useful for teaching, rebuking, correcting and training in righteousness, so that the servant of God may be thoroughly equipped for every good work.' (2 Timothy 3:16-17, NIV).

SUMMARY

Jack needs to know that the Bible is in fact the word of God. The Bible is true and trustworthy which means that what it reveals about God is the truth. We can know that God exists because the Bible tells us and we can trust the Bible.

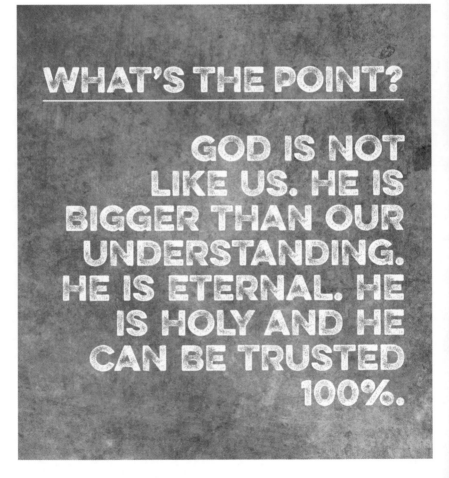

WHAT'S THE POINT?

GOD IS NOT LIKE US. HE IS BIGGER THAN OUR UNDERSTANDING. HE IS ETERNAL. HE IS HOLY AND HE CAN BE TRUSTED 100%.

IF GOD EXISTS, THEN WHAT IS HE LIKE?

(PART I)

Q: What has Jack learned about what God is like so far?

1. He has made Himself known in creating the world and the human race.
2. He speaks through the Bible.

JACK

Jack's a proud man. He likes to think of himself as self-sufficient. He doesn't need 'anybody for anything'. The only people he relies upon and trusts are his family. Even then, it's only a select few. He is suspicious of strangers and avoids anybody he thinks of as 'posh' or not 'one of the lads'. He is not a man who trusts easily.

STOP

Q: What do we think of what Jack is saying? Can we ever be truly self-sufficient or do we need other people in our lives? What are some of the dangers of trusting and not trusting people?

ILLUSTRATION

How many of us would walk up to a stranger's door and ask the person who comes to the door if they would watch over our children for 5 minutes? Would you trust a person the very first time you met them or would it take a bit of time? They would need to prove themselves, wouldn't they?

Well, the same is true for God.

How can you trust Him if you don't really know what He is like?

But, if we will only try to get to know Him better, then we will begin to see that

He can be trusted.
　He can be loved.
　　He can be followed.

Before we can get around to understanding God, we need to know that

GOD IS BIGGER THAN WE CAN EVER HOPE TO UNDERSTAND

God is so big that it is hard for us to even imagine. It's not the most imaginative illustration, and I'm not the first to use it, but a good way to begin to understand the vastness of God is to think about the universe. Most of us will get the fact that the Earth is just one planet in our solar system, orbiting the sun, our closest star. Imagine you had a spaceship that could travel at the speed of light, which is 670,616,629 mph – that's pretty fast by the way! At that speed you could circle the Earth 7 times in a second.

Starting on Earth on a journey out into space, you would pass ...

the Moon in 2 seconds (our fastest spaceship just now takes 3 days)
　Mars in 4 minutes (as opposed to 6-8 months)
　　Pluto in 5 hours (New Horizons took 9.5 years!)

That's just the edge of our solar system. To get to our next closest star you'd be travelling 4.3 years (still going at the speed of light).

At that speed, just our galaxy, the Milky Way, would take 10,000 years to cross from side to side.

At that speed, it would take 2 million years to reach our next galaxy, and 20 million years to reach the next closest cluster of galaxies.

Even then, we're only just beginning to travel the universe. It's estimated that there are 100 billion galaxies in the universe, many containing billions of stars.

The universe is enormous. Mind blown?

God made that.

He is so great that He can't get any better. That's why Christians worship God.

He has given us everything,
　　He has made everything and
　　　　He is outside of everything.

He has made us to worship Him.
He has made us to depend on Him.

GOD IS ETERNAL

Not only is God beyond our complete understanding, *He is also eternal.*

God has no beginning and no ending.
　　He cannot die.
　　　　He cannot end.

He is not like anything else in our world that is born, lives and then dies. God has always existed and always will exist.

'Lord, you have been our dwelling place
　　throughout all generations.
Before the mountains were born
　　or you brought forth the whole world,
　　from everlasting to everlasting you are God.' (Psalm 90:1-2, NIV)

What do we think the word 'everlasting' means? It means as far back as we can go and as far forward as we can go, God existed.

No one has given God life
　　and no one can take away His life.

God needs nothing outside of Himself to exist.

He is self-existent.

He is self-sufficient.

GOD IS HOLY

A man called Isaiah once had a vision of God and this is what he wrote:

'Holy, holy, holy is the Lord Almighty;
the whole earth is full of his glory.' (Isaiah 6:3, NIV).

What does that word mean to us?

To be holy means to be completely different from everything else.
It means to be set apart from all His creation.

'Who among the gods
is like you, Lord?
Who is like you —
majestic in holiness,
awesome in glory,
working wonders?' (Exodus 15:11, NIV).

God is one of a kind.
He cannot do anything bad.
He loves us perfectly.
He does not lie or break His promises.
He is completely perfect and without sin.

GOD IS RIGHTEOUS

Not only is God completely perfect and pure, He is also just and fair in everything that He says and does.

Habakkuk chapter 1 verse 13 (NIV) says this about God: *'Your eyes are too pure to look on evil; you cannot tolerate wrongdoing.'*

We need to remember that because often people will tell us that God can't be just and fair when there's so much suffering in our world. Or, how can He love people and yet send them to hell? Well, we will come to that shortly. But Exodus chapter 34 tells us that God: *'does not leave the guilty unpunished.'* Now, lots of people don't mind that maybe there's a God out there who created us – that's fine. Others don't mind that He is holy and just – that's fine too. The problem comes when we tell people that this

holy,

just,

loving,

compassionate

God

will not tolerate any sin in the world

   and will punish it

      and that includes their sin.

Now that's when people start thinking: *'Hang on a minute, mate, I don't quite like the sound of that.'*

GOD NEVER CHANGES

The fifth truth is that God *never changes*. He doesn't lose His temper like us. He doesn't change His mind about people. Read Psalm 102:25-27.

So, God is bigger than we can understand, eternal, holy, righteous and unchangeable.

By knowing this about Him we can begin to see that **we can trust Him for all things**.

He won't lie to us.

   He won't let us down.

      He won't disappoint us.

         He is stronger than us.

            He is more perfect than us.

               He is somebody we can completely rely on.

The last truth for us to think about here is maybe the most difficult one.

GOD DOES NOT NEED US AT ALL.

God is very much different than we are.

Jack needs air to breathe and food to survive. <u>God, on the other hand, doesn't need anything outside of Himself in order to survive.</u>

<u>Everything in the world needs God but God does not need anything in the world.</u>

There is nothing that God needs in order to make Him better. God sits apart from the world and from us. He is not a part of creation. Some people worship animals or trees or mother earth. But God is completely separate from everything that He has created.

This is what the Bible says about God in Acts 17:24-25:

'The God who made the world and everything in it, being Lord of heaven and earth, does not live in temples made by man, nor is he served by human hands, as though he needed anything, since he himself gives to all mankind life and breath and everything.'

Imagine if we went up to Bill Gates or the dude that owns Apple computers and said, *'Listen, here's 20p towards a cup of tea or something.'* What do you think his reaction would be? What does he need your piddling 20p for? He's got billions. He doesn't need your money. He's already got more than enough. God operates the same way. He doesn't need us for anything. He's already got it all. Everything we see, including ourselves, He made and gave to us anyway!

STOP
We read these words in Isaiah 40:12 (NIV).

'Who has measured the waters in the hollow of his hand,
or with the breadth of his hand marked off the heavens?
Who has held the dust of the earth in a basket,
or weighed the mountains on the scales
and the hills in a balance?'

What do you think the author is trying to teach us here?

MEMORY VERSE

'The God who made the world and everything in it is the Lord of heaven and earth and does not live in temples built by human hands' (Acts 17:24, NIV).

SUMMARY

Jack has tried to live his life as if the one in control has been himself. He has tried to be a self-sufficient man. But Jack has to see that God is so much bigger than he is. God is eternal. He is holy and He can be trusted. Jack begins to change how he thinks about God. He can't know everything about God but what the Bible does tell Jack is that God is good and holy.

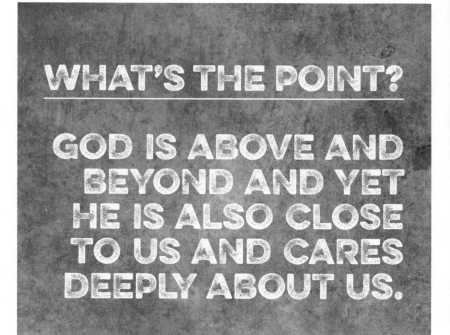

WHAT'S THE POINT?

GOD IS ABOVE AND BEYOND AND YET HE IS ALSO CLOSE TO US AND CARES DEEPLY ABOUT US.

IF GOD EXISTS, THEN WHAT IS HE LIKE?
(PART II)

JACK

Jack's had a hard life. He was born into a difficult family. His dad was abusive to his mother and his siblings. He suffered abuse at the hand of an uncle. He has lost two children at birth. Life has been brutal. How can God care about him? How can that be true? How is his life so messed up if this so-called God exists? If He is out there then He must be asleep or something. Or, maybe, it's just that God doesn't care about Jack. God is for the good people. Or maybe God just doesn't care about this world at all.

Now, because God is so far beyond our understanding, it would be easy to think of Him as somebody 'out there' or up in the skies far away from our world and our lives. In a sense these things are true. God is 'out there'. Christians say that God is

Transcendent.

Well, that's a mouthful! What does that word mean? Let's look at a Bible verse together.

> 'For my thoughts are not your thoughts,
>   neither are your ways my ways,'
> declares the LORD.
> 'As the heavens are higher than the earth,
>   so are my ways higher than your ways
>   and my thoughts than your thoughts.' (Isaiah 55:8-9, NIV)

In other words, **God exists out of space and time**.

I know. Mind blowing yet again, right? God is so above us and beyond us it is practically impossible to describe it correctly.

ILLUSTRATION

If I were to tell you what my wife was like, I could tell you her hair colour, height and skin complexion (fair). Does that adequately describe her? I could tell you she likes chocolate (in all forms). How about now? Do you know her? Not even close. If, then, I am finding it hard to explain who my wife truly is, then you can see how impossible it is to put into words God's transcendence. It is dangerous even to try, because we can easily fall into the trap of bringing God down to a human level when He is way, way above that.

Little wonder, then, that Jack views God as something completely detached from
His world and his life.

In the late 80's a singer called Nanci Griffith had a world-wide hit with the song, 'From a Distance'. The author, Julie Gold, was clear that the song was about God and how the world was not how it appeared to be. Consider her closing lyrics:

> From a distance you look like my friend,
> even though we are at war.
> From a distance I just cannot comprehend
> what all this fighting is for.
>
> From a distance there is harmony,
> and it echoes through the land.
> And it's the hope of hopes, it's the love of loves,
> it's the heart of every man.
> It's the hope of hopes; it's the love of loves.
> This is the song of every man.
> And God is watching us, God is watching us,
> God is watching us from a distance.
> Oh, God is watching us, God is watching.
> God is watching us from a distance.

These last verses sum up Jack's view of God and the world almost completely. Jack thinks, 'If God does exist, then the best we can hope for is that He is really far from us, He doesn't really care about my life'. But is this what the Bible actually teaches? <u>Is God just watching us from on high with nothing more than mild interest? Is He indifferent to our suffering? Does He care about people like Jack?</u> Listen to what the Bible says.

3

'Am I a God at hand, declares the LORD, and not a God far away?' (Jeremiah 23:23)

Many of God's enemies had the same thoughts as Jack back in the Old Testament. They even used to mock God's people that He didn't exist. They used to brag about their behaviour and show off. Listen to the Psalmist's response to the claim that God does not see what goes on in the earth.

> *'They kill the widow and the sojourner,*
> *and murder the fatherless;*
> *and they say, **"The LORD does not see;**
> **the God of Jacob does not perceive"**.'*
>
> *Understand, O dullest of the people!*
> *Fools, when will you be wise?*
>
> *He who planted the ear, does he not hear?*
> *He who formed the eye, does he not see?*
>
> *He who disciplines the nations, does he not rebuke?*
> *He who teaches man knowledge —*
> *the LORD — knows the thoughts of man,*
> *that they are but a breath.* (Psalm 94:6-11)

Even King David when he was caught in a serious sin tried to escape from the eye of the Lord. This is how he put it in one of his prayers:

'Where shall I go from your Spirit?
Or where shall I flee from your presence?
If I ascend to heaven, you are there!
If I make my bed in Sheol, you are there!
If I take the wings of the morning
and dwell in the uttermost parts of the sea,
even there your hand shall lead me,
and your right hand shall hold me.
If I say, "Surely the darkness shall cover me,
and the light about me be night,"
even the darkness is not dark to you;
the night is bright as the day,
for darkness is as light with you.' (Psalm 139:7-12)

This means that Jack **may never** find out some of the answers to the problems of his life this side of eternity.

God may be transcendent but we learn from these Bible passages that He is also close to us.

The Bible teaches us that God is
Immanent.

Yet another mouthful! What does this mean? Well, it means that even though He is above and beyond us He is also
Close to us at the same time.

God wants to be known personally.
He wants to relate to us.

This is the beginning of some good news for Jack. This means Jack can get to know God at a personal level. The Bible wasn't just written so we could know all sorts of strange facts and figures. It reveals to us that God actually wants to communicate with us. He wants to talk to us and He wants us to talk to Him. He wants to be close to us.

Now Jack is left wondering, 'Well, if God does know me, and He knows every detail of my life, then obviously He doesn't actually do anything for me; it is not as if God is involved in my life.'

But there is more.

Not only is God
    above us,
        beyond us
            and close to us.

He is also
Omniscient.

Another one of these words! Yes. And just as important as the others. It means that because God created everything He is
All knowing.

In other words, **th ere is nothing that God does not know about us**.

> 'O LORD, you have searched me and known me!
> You know when I sit down and when I rise up;
> you discern my thoughts from afar.
> You search out my path and my lying down
> and are acquainted with all my ways.
> Even before a word is on my tongue,
> behold, O LORD, you know it altogether.
> You hem me in, behind and before,
> and lay your hand upon me.
> Such knowledge is too wonderful for me;
> it is high; I cannot attain it.'

God is both near to us and far away. (Psalm 139:1-6)

God's transcendence, immanence and omniscience come together at once when we come to think about Him. In the New Testament, Paul declares that God 'himself gives to all mankind life and breath and everything' and 'in him we live and move and have our being' (Acts 17:25, 28).

God is also
Omnipotent.

This means He is **all-powerful.**

In other words, **there is nothing outside of His control**.

God guides, governs, and provides for His creation, even though He is so far above it.

3

'For all things are possible with God' (Mark 10:27, ESV).

Now even though God is different to us and separate from us, the Bible also teaches that
He is a God who draws near to us.

He has chosen to come down to us, to live amongst us, to make Himself known to us and to provide for us. We will come to this in more detail later when we look at the life of Jesus. Why would God do these things for us? It is because of our great need for Him, and not because of His great need for us. **He wants the human race to receive His goodness, His greatness, His kindness and His love**. When we enter into a relationship we try to put the other person first and meet their needs in order to try and keep them happy. That is not the way with God. There is nothing we can do to make Him happy. His love is completely unselfish. He doesn't love us because we're nice to Him or because we're so loveable. He loves us despite the fact that many of us ignore Him or pretend that He does not exist.

Q: *Do we think that we deserve to be loved by God? What's the difference between religion and what the Bible teaches us about how to find peace with God? How do you think we should respond to God's great love for us? What's stopping us then?*

MEMORY VERSE

'Am I a God at hand, declares the LORD, and not a God far away?'
(Jeremiah 23:23)

 SUMMARY

Jack's whole idea about God is utterly changed when he begins to see that *God is above and beyond us and yet He is also close to us and cares deeply about us.* It is important that Jack understands that God can be part of his life. It is possible to have a relationship with this good and holy God.

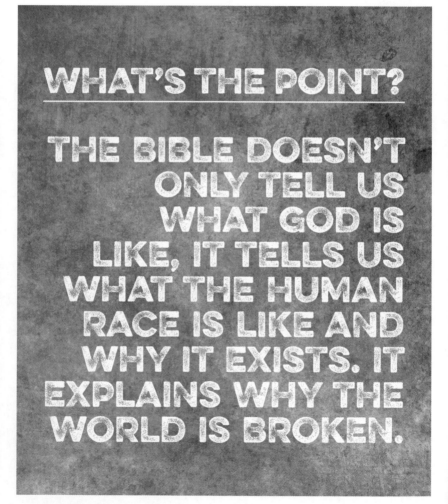

WHAT'S THE POINT?

THE BIBLE DOESN'T ONLY TELL US WHAT GOD IS LIKE, IT TELLS US WHAT THE HUMAN RACE IS LIKE AND WHY IT EXISTS. IT EXPLAINS WHY THE WORLD IS BROKEN.

IF GOD EXISTS, WHAT DOES IT HAVE TO DO WITH ME?

JACK

Jack knows the world is broken. His whole life is a mess. He doesn't need to be convinced of that. When we ask Jack how he thinks the world got to be like it is, he doesn't have an answer. He thinks it's because people are greedy and selfish but he's not sure of much else. He doesn't agree with abortion. He thinks that's 'wrong' but he's not sure why. He thinks that there should be the death penalty for perverts but that other criminals are not as bad. He thinks of himself as 'good' in that he loves his family, although he cheats on his wife ('I can't help it') and sells recreational drugs regularly ('I need the money and I'm not harming anybody'). He thinks that bankers are all thieves and should be punished but he thinks nothing of making false claims to the social security. Everybody's doing it (read everybody he knows) and what's the harm? Jack is a victim and in his mind he is only making the best out of the hand life has dealt him.

STOP

What do we think about Jack's view of the world and himself? What do we think is wrong with the world? What do we think needs to be done to make it right?

WHY WE ARE HERE

If Genesis 1 reminds us that we have been made in the image of God, it also informs us why God has done this.

Evolution teaches that life is pointless

but the Bible teaches us that life is purposeful.

Our true purpose in life is to represent the God who made us. How do we do that?

1. By worshipping God correctly
2. By having a correct understanding of our place in the world
3. By living in relationship to other people
4. By subduing and having dominion over the rest of creation.

1. WORSHIPPING GOD

According to the Westminster Shorter Catechism, the main purpose for which we were made is:

to glorify God, and to enjoy him forever.

'We were made to worship.
     It is hardwired into our systems.
Even the worship of nothing is the worship of something.
     Some of us worship our children.
Some of us worship our jobs.
     Some of us worship our drugs.'

But we were created for so much more than that. A key part of worship is **obedience**.

OBEYING GOD

We discover the Garden of Eden in Genesis 2:8. Everybody has heard of the Garden of Eden. The word means 'delight' or *'pleasure'*. It was a place of wonder. In fact it was the most beautiful place in all of creation. It was there that God and man walked in perfect harmony. Adam and Eve had full and open access to God at any time. It is in this place that God gave a clear command to man in verses 16-17 (NIV):

'And the Lord God commanded the man, "You are free to eat from any tree in the garden; but you must not eat from the tree of the knowledge of good and evil, for when you eat from it you will certainly die".'

So, even though God and man were at peace with one another, God clearly put boundaries in place that He expected to be followed. **This rule was a way of reminding him never to forget that he was the created and God was the creator.** Even in paradise there were boundaries to be respected and, more importantly, obeyed.

ILLUSTRATION

We have all seen road signs as we are travelling down the motorway. They warn us of speed limits and sometimes of dangers up ahead. We have all seen 'Keep Out' signs on the outside of building sites and private property. They are there as a warning to us. Observe them – or there will be consequences. That is what was going on in Eden. What the Bible records in Genesis is the great test of obedience.

Adam had everything in paradise – everything – except this one thing – this one thing that reminded him that he was subject to God, not equal to Him and certainly not better than Him. God gave Adam a command and he could choose the good option – obedience – or he could disobey God – evil.

So at the beginning we had man and woman, created in God's image, living in a lush paradise with every need provided for and with full access to God. All they had to do was obey and trust in God completely to know what was best for their lives.

2. UNDERSTANDING OUR PLACE IN THE WORLD

We were created by God *to be His image-bearers.* But, what does that actually mean?

ILLUSTRATION

Some have used images to govern by fear. Many of us will remember Saddam Hussein. Because Iraq was such a large country and almost impossible to govern personally, he had loads of statues – images – of himself built and placed around the whole country. There would be pictures of him on every street corner and in all the businesses to remind people who was in charge – who was the boss. So, when he was finally removed from power, there was great significance in the pulling down of these statues because they signified the end of his rule and authority over them as a people.

Likewise, many kingdoms in the Ancient Near East stretched across thousands of square miles. The kings of these empires were powerful leaders, but the size of their kingdoms presented serious political problems. How could kings exercise control over their empires? How could they keep order? Ancient kings simply could not maintain personal contact with all regions of their nations. They needed other ways to establish their authority. Many rulers solved this problem by erecting images of themselves at key sites throughout their kingdoms. They produced numerous statues of themselves and endowed their images with representative authority. As we gaze upon the remains of these imposing figures, their ancient purpose becomes evident. When citizens saw the images of their emperor, they understood to whom they owed their allegiance. They knew for certain who ruled the land.

When God says, *'Multiply yourselves'* what He really means is, *'I want my images spread to the ends of the world.'* He didn't want to multiply His image because He feared losing control like these earthly rulers, but rather because He wanted us to rule well, imitating His goodness. God commanded His image-bearers to reign over the earth. *'Subdue and rule'*, God commanded, *'I give you authority to represent me in my world.'* We are special creatures, lovingly made and with a unique role in the world as God's image-bearers and representatives. It is the highest calling. There is none higher.

3. CREATED TO RELATE TO OTHERS

God decided that it wasn't good for Adam to live alone and so He created Eve for him. That's why we read in Genesis 2:18 *that it was not good for man to be alone.* Men and women were made not only to relate to God but to each other.

CHAPTER 5

4. AUTHORITY OVER CREATION

But it didn't stop there. God did not only say 'multiply' to Adam and Eve, but 'have dominion'. That means as image-bearers they had a responsibility to look after the earth. Listen to how the Psalmist puts it in Psalm 8:6-8,

> 'You have given him dominion over the works of your hands; you have put all things under his feet, all sheep and oxen, and also the beasts of the field, the birds of the heavens, and the fish of the sea, whatever passes along the paths of the seas.'

The whole issue of naming is an important cultural issue that we need to understand. Notice who does the naming. It is important. Man will name all of the things over which he has dominion – plants, animals etc. God on the other hand, names day, night, heavens, earth, sea and man. Why? Because, ultimately, He controls all of these things. Man cannot control the elements – he can only try to adapt to them as best he can. Only God can control these other things.

Adam was the world's first and best human scientist.

In the Old Testament 'to name' means to express the true nature of a thing. The point is that he didn't just pick the name for things out of the air. He would have known the nature and function of each animal and given it the appropriate name. He was a smart cookie! People often ask me what language he spoke but I don't have a clue. He could have had a broad Scottish brogue for all I know! Some ask about how he could possibly have named all the species in one day, had a big nap, woman was made and then he named her as well. Well there is a debate over whether we use the word 'kinds' or 'species'. Don't worry about it. Let's say Adam could reasonably name ten a minute – he could easily name three thousand types of animal within five hours. There are many questions and there are many solutions.

Nor was Adam created just to potter about and do a spot of sunbathing. Adam was given a special commission by God Himself to tend the garden – to guard over it. So work was a God-given command before the Fall. We have not been created for idleness and leisure but for work, activity and service.

Eden was a perfect paradise where man walked with God, he had plenty to eat, he worked and he had Eve. What a life! There was what the Bible calls true *shalom* in the world. There was perfection, completeness, welfare and peace at every level of society between the creation and the creator.

JACK

Hang on a minute. That sounds a bit like a fairy story. We all lived in a nice garden and God hangs out with us. But, the world isn't like that, is it? Where's God now then? Why doesn't He show Himself? Why all these problems and suffering in the world if He is so kind and good?

Q: What do you think the answer is? How have we gone from peace and perfection to the mess we live in today?

Jacks' right. There is a problem. But the problem of the world isn't a problem with God. The problem of the world is a problem with us. The world is broken. It is not as it should be. Even Jack sees that. How has this mess happened? For the answer to that, we have to return to Eden. The world is not like that anymore.

Something happened to destroy this paradise...

SUMMARY

Jack knows that the world is messed up and it is not the way it ought to be. He now starts to see that he was actually made for something; his life has a reason, God created all people to enjoy Him forever yet this has not been his experience. Now, for the first time, he begins to wonder how he can have this kind of relationship with God.

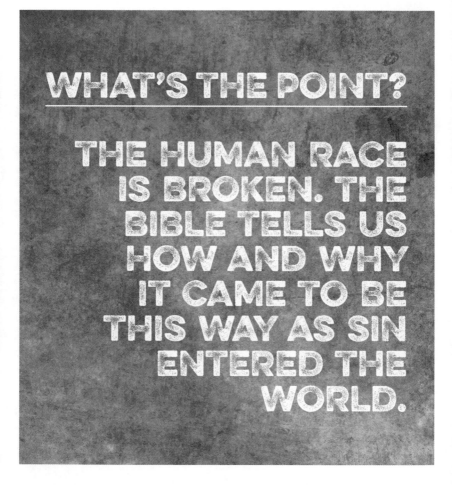

WHAT'S THE POINT?

THE HUMAN RACE IS BROKEN. THE BIBLE TELLS US HOW AND WHY IT CAME TO BE THIS WAY AS SIN ENTERED THE WORLD.

IF GOD EXISTS, THEN WHAT'S WRONG WITH OUR WORLD?

3

BIBLE

Now the serpent was more crafty than any other beast of the field that the Lord God had made. He said to the woman, 'Did God actually say, "You shall not eat of any tree in the garden"?' And the woman said to the serpent, 'We may eat of the fruit of the trees in the garden, but God said, "You shall not eat of the fruit of the tree that is in the midst of the garden, neither shall you touch it, lest you die".' But the serpent said to the woman, 'You will not surely die. For God knows that when you eat of it your eyes will be opened, and you will be like God, knowing good and evil.' So when the woman saw that the tree was good for food, and that it was a delight to the eyes, and that the tree was to be desired to make one wise, she took of its fruit and ate, and she also gave some to her husband who was with her, and he ate. Then the eyes of both were opened, and they knew that they were naked. And they sewed fig leaves together and made themselves loincloths (Genesis 3:1-7).

THE FALL

Adam and Eve were told not to eat of the fruit from the tree of knowledge of good and evil. It seems like such a simple rule, right? It was there to remind them that they were not gods. There was only one God and they were to live under His rule. So, when Eve took the fruit and gave it to Adam she was rebelling against God and declaring her independence. They didn't accidentally bump into the tree and some fruit fell to the ground which they thought they would stick in a curry so as not to have any waste. They knew what they were doing was wrong. They knew that they were going against God's command. They wilfully rebelled. Sin entered their hearts and entered the world. That's what sin is.

Wilful rebellion against God and His rule.

Adam and Eve denied and defied their creator.

THE RESULTS OF THE FALL

What happens next is tragic. Adam and Eve are expelled from the presence of God in Eden.

A death sentence now hangs over them.

They would have to toil in their work and, ultimately, they would die. Of course they lived for a few hundred years (in their case) but they would be physically and spiritually separated from God for eternity.

Romans 5:12-21 teaches that through the one sin of the one man, Adam,
> Sin entered the world
>> Death entered the world
>>> Death came to all men
> Death reigned
>> Many die by the trespass of the one man
>>> The judgement followed one sin
> And brought condemnation
>> Death reigned through one man
>>> Condemnation for all men
> Many were made sinners
>> Sin reigned in death.

Because of their sin, **we too are now under God's condemnation**. We too are separated from Him. **The penalty of physical and spiritual death hangs over us**.

That means, because of the Fall everything has been shattered. All of our peace has gone. And we see it in many ways.

People no longer worship God.

In fact they ignore Him and deny His existence. They look for any other reason they can to say how we got here as long as they don't have to give God any credit.

We hate God.
We worship anything but Him.

For Jack that meant worshipping money. That's what got him out of bed in the morning. He would do whatever it took to make money. Even if it meant hurting people. Jack (although he didn't know it) worshipped drugs. They were what he thought about when he got up, went about his day and went to bed. They made him happy. They filled his life. They got him through his day.

People are a mess

There is no peace in Jack's life. He feels empty. He feels like it is all just pointless. His friends don't have any answers. Drugs haven't made him happy. They've ruined every relationship he's ever had. They've turned him into a zombie. He doesn't really have an inner peace. He feels angry all the time and he doesn't know why. He feels restless all the time. He's never satisfied. He always wants more.

Relationships are a mess

Jack says that his family are the most important thing but it doesn't stop him cheating on his wife. It doesn't stop him blowing the food money on drugs. His family are embarrassed because he is always in trouble with the law. His neighbours are scared of him because of his volatile nature. There is no peace in Jack's world. He talks about community but he lives to exploit others. Screw them before they screw me is how he lives his life.

Jack is feeling the full effects of the Fall many thousands of years after it happened.

Because sin entered the world through Adam, all of us now suffer.

JACK
Hang on. They did that. It wasn't me, was it? What's it got to do with me? How can that be fair? Why should I have to suffer for what they did?

Good questions.

ILLUSTRATION

If a drug addict takes heroin while pregnant, that will have devastating effects on her unborn child. If a man loses his job, gets drunk and beats his wife in frustration in front of his watching children, is that fair on them? We are born with certain traits of our human parents, even physical defects. In the same way we are born with the spiritual defects of our ancestors. We are born spiritually blind and slaves to sin. We sin because we are born sinners. Every single part of the human race has been affected by sin. Every part of us has been affected by the Fall. We are not completely bad. We are capable of good and kind acts. But we are completely tainted by sin. It doesn't matter whether we were in the garden or not. We have been affected by the Fall and we only have to look at our own lives and the world around us to see the truth of this. The Fall has devastated our world.

Adam acts as the representative for all humanity when he fell into sin. Romans 5:15 is clear about this; *it is by one man's offence that many died.*

The universal problem of death in the world is traced all the way back to the initial sin of one man.

ILLUSTRATION

Imagine an ambassador in another country. He is constantly acting on behalf of the interests of his country. He is the representative of each citizen of that country. When he speaks he speaks for them all. When he acts he acts for them all. The idea here is the same.

God has appointed Adam as the representative of the human race. He was told plainly as our representative that if he disobeyed God he would die, and the implication was that we who follow him would also die. He disobeyed and thus brought judgement upon us all. **Adam sinned and we all sinned**.

Get this! The whole human race is guilty because of this one sin of Adam.

It is not our own sin that makes us sinners. It is the sin of the original representative of the human race that makes us sinners. He stood, and fell, for us all. It may not sound fair to Jack but it is the truth nonetheless.

ILLUSTRATION

You are playing footie in the street with your pal and you hit a wayward shot and smash your neighbour's window. Your neighbour comes out and asks your dad to foot the bill. Even though your dad didn't break the window he bears the responsibility for the offence because you are unable to.

JACK

But how is that fair? How can it be fair if I am only a sinner because of Adam?

Jack needs to know that he is not only born a sinner. He is not only one by nature but he is also a sinner by choice.

> He chooses to steal.
>> He chooses to cheat on his wife.
>>> He chooses to deal drugs.
>>>> He chooses to ignore the Bible.
>>>>> He chooses to live life on his own terms.

Jack is a lawbreaker in the eyes of God.

JACK AND THE LAW

Jack decides to change his approach. He thinks to himself, *'OK. I have been in trouble with the law as far back as I can remember. Rules are there to be broken. Everybody breaks the law. So, why shouldn't I? Anyway, it's not like I'm a paedophile, is it? That's who God should be punishing. Not people like me, right?'*

Q: What do we think? Is Jack right or wrong?

Now the book of Romans is hardcore for a number of reasons. Many of us are like Jack, for **we see ourselves as victims**. Maybe we had a bad childhood. Maybe life has kicked us up and down the street a bit. Maybe many of us like to excuse our behaviour by blaming others or our circumstances. You know, the usual excuse is *'Well, I had to smash that fella* *in the face cause he owed me money. It's not my fault, they made me do it.'* But the Bible doesn't give us an opt out. In fact, particularly in the book of Romans, it does the exact opposite.

In this book, Paul tells his readers that we are responsible for our actions before God, however hard or easy life has been for us. So none of us are victims when it comes to obeying God. The Bible is clear about this. And in fact, in Romans 3:23 we learn that,

> *'...all have sinned and fall short of the glory of God.'*

It gets worse.

Listen to Romans 1:18 (NIV),

> *'The wrath of God is being revealed from heaven against [those]... who suppress the truth'.*

In other words, the Bible says we are truth suppressors.

In other words, we know deep down inside that God exists, it's just that we choose to ignore Him and live life in our own way and on our own terms. We literally hold the truth down. We don't want to hear it and we don't even want to think about it. It's like when we fall out with somebody; often we will deny their very existence. We will say to friends and family, so-and-so is dead to me and we'll blank them in the street, usually we'll unfriend them from Facebook. Of course, we know they exist, we're just denying them. That is how the Bible describes what we do to God. We know He exists – and creation all around us proves it – we just blank Him and deny His very existence.

We suppress the truth about Him.

> After all nobody is going to tell us how to live our lives!
> We will do what we like, when we like!

And that is just what we do.

So the Bible says, <u>we are born sinners and we stay sinners as we walk through life doing our own thing and giving no thought to God whatsoever.</u> Some people say, 'Well I didn't know. Nobody told me that God existed.' But listen to what Paul says in Romans 1:19-23. He says: 'For what can be known about God is plain to them' (he's talking about the human race), 'because God has shown it to them. For his invisible attributes, namely, his eternal power and divine nature, have been clearly perceived, ever since the creation of the world, in the things that have been made. So they are without excuse.' People, he says, 'have exchanged the glory of the immortal God for images resembling mortal man and birds and animals and creeping things.'

We are without excuse.

The Bible does not let us off the hook however much we like to wriggle.

So it's not that we don't know. It's that we push the truth of God's existence to the back of our minds.

Or we don't care enough to think deeply about it.

We've all wondered, haven't we, at one point or another how we got here or who made the world? And we've all come up with our own wild and wacky ideas to explain it away. <u>The Bible says that we can tell from creation around us that God exists, but we choose to believe in lies instead.</u>

After all, why believe in a God we have to obey when we can believe in evolution? Then we don't have to do anything about it, do we? We don't have to be responsible. We don't have to be obedient. Why believe that life makes sense and we have to do something when we can just pretend it's all a big accident and none of it matters?

> But deep down inside when the lights are off, and when all our friends have gone home, we know that life matters.

We know that people matter.

We know in the deep dark recesses of our souls that there's a Creator out there.

Paul says we're rebels by nature. What does that mean? It means this: we don't like authority! It doesn't matter whether it's the police, the government or the telephone company. We do not like being told what to do. The book of Romans tells us that no one honours God, nobody gives thanks to Him as they should. And it says that although we know that God is God and He should be worshipped, we worship other things instead. **This is an insult to God**.

Paul makes it clear that **everyone is a sinner**, **everyone has rebelled against God**. We will all stand before God, the righteous Judge, and none of us have a leg to stand on — we'll all be held accountable. We're in deep, deep trouble. All of us. We've got to be clear about that. And here's the scarier news, there's not a single thing we can do about it. It doesn't matter what we say, what we do, what we promise ourselves or our loved ones, we are powerless to change our lives and our standing before God Almighty.

The Bible is clear, we will go to our graves in our sin and we will have to face a holy and mighty God.

This is how the author to the Hebrews describes it in chapter 9 and verse 27 (NIV), '...people are destined to die once, and after that to face judgment'.

We will have no defence against God's charges.
We are guilty and we will be sentenced to an eternity outside of God's presence in hell.

The Bible makes this very, very clear indeed.

The problem with Jack is that he has misunderstood sin. He thinks it's just about breaking **the law of the land**. So, little laws get little punishment and big ones get big punishment. In that view of the law everybody gets what he or she deserves.

But in God's view of sin everybody is a lawbreaker regardless of what they have done.

Jack has to realise that he has not lived for God. He does not worship God. He has not honoured his wife. He's lived life by his own rules. He has done things his own way. It has not got him very far. He is deeply unhappy and unsatisfied with his life. But that's not his biggest problem.

His biggest problem is that the God who made him is unhappy with him.

He is a sinner.
He is a rebel against God and His authority.

Therefore, God is angry with him and his sin.

All sinners stand on an equal footing before God.

Q: Given what we know about him, has Jack been holy? Has he obeyed God? Is he working for the glory of God? Is he living life for the reasons God created him? Is Jack a sinner by the Bible's definition? If so, then what does that mean for him?

3

The Bible tells us that God hates sin:
'The LORD passed before him and proclaimed, "The LORD, the LORD, a God merciful and gracious, slow to anger, and abounding in steadfast love and faithfulness, keeping steadfast love for thousands, forgiving iniquity and transgression and sin, but who will by no means clear the guilty, visiting the iniquity of the fathers on the children and the children's children, to the third and the fourth generation"' (Exodus 34:6-7)

PUNISHMENT FOR SIN

Sin has to be punished. The problem is that when we talk of God punishing sin many people get upset. They claim it is unfair and unjust for God to punish sinners. Where is the love in that?

Now, we don't think parents are unloving when they punish their children for disobedience. We don't think it's wrong when rapists get sent to prison for their crimes. Yet, somehow people believe that God would no longer be loving if He were to punish people for their wrongdoing. But of course that's not true. **A loving God will punish wickedness**. The problem isn't really that we think it's wrong to punish certain types of people. The problem is that we don't think that we deserve to be punished because we're not as bad as so and so. Too many of us think we will get away with being judged by God because, you know what — we're alright at heart. We might have done the odd shady thing in life but nothing too heavy. So, God is going to let us off the hook at the end of the day. But we would be dead wrong to think like this.

Jack needs to realise that he was born a sinner. As soon as he was able, Jack sinned. Jack deserves death. All sinners do. He is in big trouble. He thought his biggest problem was his addictions. But he just found out that his biggest problem is that God is angry with him and because of his sin he is separated from Him and has a one-way ticket to hell.

Hell is not a topic that people like talking about or thinking about anymore. Even Christians find it uncomfortable or even offensive that God would send people to hell. He's all about love, right? Well the Bible says that it is destined for man to die once and then to face the judgement of God (Hebrews 9:27). And if the Bible warns us against hell, why should we try to make it more acceptable or water it down to make the message sound a little bit easier? Why would we comfort sinners with the thought that maybe hell won't be as bad as the Bible tells us it is or maybe it doesn't exist really?

We have seen that the human race has a serious sin problem and it will have to be dealt with in a serious manner. Every court in the world will sentence criminals according to how severe the crime is.

So God, who is the ultimate judge, will pass the highest sentence on sin.

Why?

Because it is the greatest offence against Him and His holy nature.

So Christians didn't make hell up to scare you into going to church or into giving money to the church. We simply believe the Bible. We believe it when it says that hell is real. We believe it with tears when we say that people we love are in danger of spending eternity there.

People will mock the thought of God today. Many will reject Him outright. Many others will murder Christians.

But one day every single one of us will die and we will meet our Maker. And we will stand before Him to give an account for our lives.

We will stand before the only Judge who matters and we will have to recognise His authority then whether we want to or not.

There will be no right of appeal.
There will be no plea-bargaining.

There will be a simple pronouncement of either guilty or not guilty; and **if we are guilty we will be condemned for all of eternity.**

That is very bad news. Very bad news indeed...

'If this is all true then I am in real trouble,' says Jack. *'What am I going to do now?'*

Well, this is where Jesus comes into the picture. Here comes some good news.

SUMMARY

Jack has to see that he has not lived for God and that his biggest problem is that he does not worship God. He's lived life by his own rules and that is why his life seems so messed up. He is deeply unhappy and unsatisfied with his life and God is unhappy with him. Jack understands now that he is a sinner, a lawbreaker, in the eyes of God. He is guilty and will be condemned for all of eternity. That is very bad news.

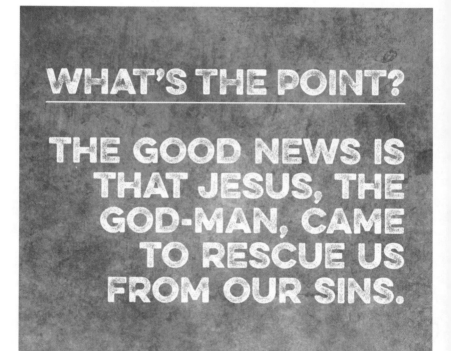

WHAT'S THE POINT?

THE GOOD NEWS IS THAT JESUS, THE GOD-MAN, CAME TO RESCUE US FROM OUR SINS.

IF GOD EXISTS, WHAT'S JESUS GOT TO DO WITH IT?

JACK

Of course Jack has heard of Jesus Christ. His family are Catholics and there are a few pictures of Him hanging about in his Nan's bedroom. *'He was like the Son of God or something,'* mumbles Jack. *'He died for our sins and He loves everybody.'* He doesn't understand much more than that. He believes that Jesus was crucified but has no idea what any of it means and how it has any relevance to his life. How is this good news for him? How does it help him if God is angry with him and his sin? How is Jesus going to be any help?

UNDERSTANDING THE GOOD NEWS OF JESUS

In the Bible the word used for 'good news' is 'gospel'. But, what exactly is the gospel and what does it have to do with Jesus? Listen to how Paul explains this good news to the church in 1 Corinthians 15:1-5.

'Now I would remind you, brothers, of the gospel I preached to you, which you received, in which you stand, and by which you are being saved, if you hold fast to the word I preached to you – unless you believed in vain. For I delivered to you as of first importance what I also received: that Christ died for our sins in accordance with the Scriptures, that he was buried, that he was raised on the third day in accordance with the Scriptures, and that he appeared to Cephas, then to the twelve.'

The first thing we must realise from the off is that this good news is not about us.

It is for us, but not about us.

It is all about Jesus,
> His life,
>> His death
>>> and His resurrection.

Now one of the best places to look for a basic explanation of the gospel is in this book called Romans. It's actually a letter written by the Apostle Paul to a group of Christians in Rome that he'd never met, explaining the importance of the good news of Jesus. In chapters 1-4 Paul gives us a detailed explanation of the gospel. In 1:1 he calls it, '...the gospel of God.' He says in 1:16, 'I am not ashamed of the gospel, for it is the power of God for salvation to everyone who believes.' The Apostle Paul says that God's solution to our sin

is the sacrificial death and resurrection of Jesus Christ.

This is the good news.
This is the *gospel* of Jesus.

Jesus is not like us.
Jesus is perfect.
Jesus is without sin.

Jesus fully and completely obeys God the Father as He lived and died among us. In Romans 3:21 Paul calls Jesus, '...the righteousness of God'. In other words, the only way a person can get right with God and avoid the punishment of eternal hell is to be completely righteous.

Jack had always thought that people who go to church were people who thought that they were better than everyone else, 'do-gooders' trying to buy God's love. But we know that can't be done. Like Jack, we are sinners. We cannot get right with God by being religious. It doesn't matter if we study the Bible or if we go to church every Sunday. Those might be good things but they do not make us right with God. The only way we can get right with God and avoid eternal punishment is found in the gospel.

Jack is confused. You see, up until now, he had always thought that people who go to church had got their life straightened out, that you had to be good and do good things for God to accept you. What the Bible actually tells us is that there's a way for us to be right with God that's got absolutely nothing to do with living as a 'good' person. That way is through Jesus' sacrificial death and resurrection. The Bible says we are: *'justified by his grace as a gift, through the redemption that is in Christ Jesus'* (Romans 3:24). So because of His life and sacrificial death, sinful mankind can be saved from the punishment that our sins deserve. And finally, Paul tells his readers how they can be included in this salvation. It is, *'through faith in Jesus Christ'*, which is *'for all who believe'* (Romans 3:22).

We're saved by trusting in Jesus and no other.

Sin is serious.
But the end result of sin — eternal separation from God in hell — is brutal.

God could have left us to our own devices indefinitely. We want to live life on our own terms and so He could have just shrugged His shoulders and left us to it. And some of us probably think that's exactly what He has done. We think He doesn't care about people like us. We think He's only interested in good people or religious people or people who go to church on Sundays. And to many of us it sounds mad that the God who made everything in the whole known world would do anything for us. But He has done something. God has not left us on our own but actually made a way for us to be rescued from the penalty of sin. God has stepped in Himself to sort out our sin problem.

And this is where Jesus comes in. We need to understand that Jesus is not God's Plan B. This isn't God panicking because we didn't behave ourselves.

Ever since the Garden of Eden, there has been hope that God would provide a rescuer for the human race. That's why way back in Genesis 3:15 we read this prophecy about Jesus which God told the serpent. It says, *'he shall bruise your head, and you shall bruise his heel.'* Now that's a strange sounding part of the Bible but, basically, what's going on is this:

Satan and his demons will be at war with humanity. But one day Jesus will come and crush Satan and He will bring this war to an end as He defeats all the forces of evil on the cross.

The rest of the Bible tells us the story of how God prepared the world through the Law and the Prophets for this stunning victory against the devil, sin and death in the life, death and resurrection of Jesus Christ. Again listen to these words from the Bible, this time in Isaiah chapter 9:6-7, we read:

'For to us a child is born, to us a son is given; and the government shall be upon his shoulder, and his name shall be called Wonderful Counsellor, Mighty God, Everlasting Father, Prince of Peace. Of the increase of his government and of peace there will be no end, on the throne of David and over his kingdom, to establish it and to uphold it with justice and with righteousness from this time forth and forevermore. The zeal of the Lord of hosts will do this.'

This is just one of God's many promises that teach us Jesus would one day put an end to the world's evil and rescue people from their sin. Through Jesus God would sweep away all resistance and establish His rule and His kingdom over all the earth.

As much as the Old Testament points to Jesus, the New Testament explains the good news of His life, death and resurrection. So Mark's gospel begins by saying: *'The beginning of the gospel of Jesus Christ, the Son of God.'* Mark knew that the coming of Jesus was the good news to a world so devastated by sin.

The other three gospels in the New Testament – Matthew, Luke and John – leave us in no doubt that Jesus was not an ordinary man. **He was both completely man and completely God**. And this is important because only someone who is both fully God and fully man would be able to save us from our sins.

If Jesus wasn't God, He would not have been perfectly righteous, no more able to save us than one dead man trying to save another. But if He wasn't fully man, then He wouldn't have been able to represent us before Almighty God and *'sympathise with our weaknesses'* having been *'tempted, as we are, yet without sin'* (Hebrews 4:15). Jesus knew why He had come to earth. In Mark 10:45 (NIV) He says: *'the Son of Man did not come to be served, but to serve, and to give his life as a ransom for many.'* Jesus knew exactly why He was going to die.

His death would buy back the lost souls of those who turn to Him in repentance and faith.

In His death He was paying the price that sin deserved.

Christ's followers in the early church also knew this to be true. Paul puts it like this in 2 Corinthians 5:21 (NIV), *'God made him who had no sin to be sin for us, so that in him we might become the righteousness of God'.* In 1 Peter 3:18 (NIV) we learn that *'Christ also suffered once for sins, the righteous for the unrighteous, to bring you to God. He was put to death in the body but made alive in the Spirit.'* In other words, **when Jesus died, He wasn't being punished for His own sin because He didn't have any**. It was actually the punishment for His people's sins.

And as Jesus hung on the cross, He cried out *'My God, my God, why have you forsaken me?'* (Matthew 27:46). And God the Father, who is both holy and righteous, whose eyes are too pure to look upon evil, looked at His Son, saw the sins of His people resting on His shoulders, and turned away in disgust and poured out His full and terrible wrath on Jesus.

Jack had seen the cross hanging on his Nan's kitchen wall and he even used to wear a cross around his neck when he was a teenager for good luck, but he had no idea that the cross was more than a good luck charm. The cross means something far more for Jack than he ever imagined. On that cross, 2,000 years ago, an innocent man was slaughtered because of Jack's own sin.

Now for some people this is the hardest and most hated part of the gospel – the idea that Jesus would be punished for someone else's sin. Some people call this *'divine child abuse'*. But, if we throw out penal substitution, then we end up with so many unanswered questions, like: Why the point of sacrifices? What did the shedding of blood accomplish? How can God have mercy on sinners without destroying justice? What does it mean that God forgives sin, but doesn't clear the guilty (Exodus 34:7)? How can a righteous and holy God justify the ungodly (Romans 4:5)?

Well the answer to all these questions is found in the cross of Jesus and in His substitutionary death for His people. In Jesus' death, God's wrath and justice are satisfied, and His mercy can be poured out. Now that's a heavy, heavy message but being hard and being difficult doesn't make it untrue.

This is all good news because Jesus is no longer dead. He rose from the grave.

Now if Christ were still dead, everything He claimed would have been meaningless, humanity would still be without hope of being saved from our sin. But we know that on the third day Jesus rose again. Paul glories in this truth. In Romans 8:33-35, we read: *'Who shall bring any charge against God's elect? It is God who justifies. Who is to condemn? Christ Jesus is the one who died – more than that, who was raised – who is at the right hand of God, who indeed is interceding for us. Who shall separate us from the love of Christ?'*

And Jesus now sits in glory at the right hand of the Father in heaven reigning as the King of the universe, and He is praying for His people even now as we await His return in glory.

SUMMARY

Jack now knows that he is a sinner and is guilty before God. Yet God sent Jesus, His Son, to live a perfect sinless life and to die the death of a sinner on the cross. He was condemned and judged as guilty just as Jack should be condemned and punished. Jesus died as Jack's substitute but because Jesus is God He defeated death and rose from the grave. He lives today. Up until now Jesus had been a part of ancient history but now all of a sudden Jack sees Jesus as someone relevant to him now.

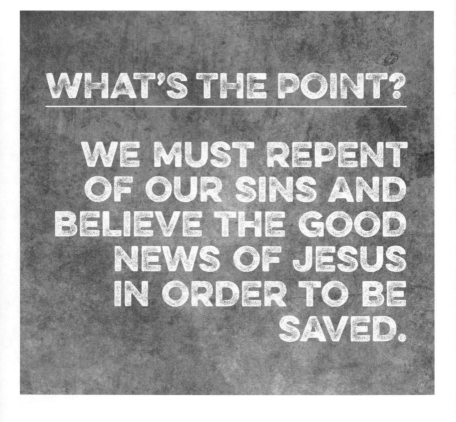

WHAT'S THE POINT?

WE MUST REPENT OF OUR SINS AND BELIEVE THE GOOD NEWS OF JESUS IN ORDER TO BE SAVED.

IF ALL THIS IS TRUE, NOW WHAT?

The good news about Jesus requires a response from us. In Mark 1:15, Jesus says:

'The time is fulfilled, and the kingdom of God is at hand; repent and believe in the gospel.'

So, God wants us to do two things in response to this good news of Jesus. He wants us to

(1) repent
    and
(2) believe.

In really simple terms, a **Christian is just a person**

**who has believed the good news about Jesus
and
repented of their sin.**

But, what exactly does that look like?

FAITH

Faith is a word that's so misused in our culture. Most people have no idea what it really means. So if we were to ask Jack about faith, he would connect it to belief in the ridiculous. So for instance, he would connect faith to children believing in Santa Claus and the Easter Bunny. He would say mystics have faith when they believe in the power of their healing stones and crystals. He would say crazy people have faith when they believe in fairies. He would equate Christian faith with all of these other things when they mentioned faith in Jesus Christ. For Jack, faith is merely how a person feels about certain things, whether they are true or not. Faith is *whatever works for you*.

Now that idea of faith is just not found in the Bible. Biblically speaking, faith is **not** believing in something that you can't prove. Biblically faith is based on

> **reliable**
> **rock-solid**
> **truth**
> > **all centred around**
> > > **the gospel of the risen Lord Jesus Christ.**

As we've seen, our greatest need as human beings is to be found righteous in God's sight, to be declared not guilty. The Bible uses the word **'justified'** — **when God declares us righteous in His sight, and not guilty**. Therefore, when we put our faith in Jesus we're relying on Jesus alone to provide us with a righteous verdict from God the Judge, instead of a guilty one. We can't be righteous in our own strength, by the things we do or don't do. If God is ever going to count us righteous, it's not going to be on the basis of our good behaviour — it's going to need to be on the basis of somebody else's record.

That's where faith in Jesus comes in.

> **In His perfect life and His death on the cross, Jesus is our substitute who stands in our place.**

> **He stands before God, His perfect record becomes ours, and so God declares us righteous.**

So when we trust in Jesus to save us, we become united to Him, and a great exchange takes place.

All of our rebellion, sin and wickedness is imputed, or credited, to Jesus and He dies because of it.

At the same time, Jesus' perfect life is imputed to us, and we are declared righteous by God. So instead of God seeing our sin, He looks at us and sees the perfect righteousness of His Son.

The Bible is clear that we are fully dependent **on Jesus alone for our salvation**. There is no other way, there is no other saviour, and there is nothing in the world that we can rely on for our salvation.

JACK

So, let me get this right. You are saying that in order for us to have peace with God we just need to have faith in Jesus? That's it? Surely, there's more to it than that? What about going to church and being good? That must count for something?

Q: What do you think? Where is Jack right and where is he wrong based on what we've learned so far?

The problem Jack has is that by believing he can be good enough to please God he is actually making a big mistake. It's a mistake a lot of people make and it's a trap that most religions fall into.

We cannot be saved by anything good that we do.

In fact, it doesn't matter how good we are or how many good deeds we do, we cannot please God that way.

We can never do enough to make God happy with us.

The Bible teaches us that our salvation is **a gift of grace**. Therefore **we do not contribute anything to it at all**. Trusting in Jesus means exactly that. We trust in Jesus and that is it. End of story. Nothing more. Nothing less. **Faith rests in Jesus and Jesus alone**.

What then is repentance?

REPENTANCE

Repentance is **turning away from sin** and **wrongdoing, hating it, and choosing, by God's strength to leave it behind**. Repentance is not an optional extra in the Christian life. Repentance is absolutely crucial to it. It shows those who have been saved by God and those who haven't. So we need to have faith in Jesus as our Saviour, and follow Him as our Lord – we can't be a follower of Christ and have one without the other.

Repentance is saying no to sin in our lives. It is running as fast and as far away as we can from the sin in our lives that would keep us from God. It is turning from our sin and turning to Christ again and again every time we find ourselves in trouble.

Repentance doesn't mean that Christians never sin.

We never stop sinning completely in this life. We will always battle with sin. Christians are not perfect this side of heaven. And every Christian will struggle with the battle against sin throughout their lives. The key word here is

Struggle

Sinful things that we once enjoyed doing no longer hold the same attraction to us. We find that we have no peace in our hearts where once we weren't too bothered.

JACK

What do you mean by that? Does that mean I have to stop going to the pub with the lads? Do I have to stop drinking and all that?

Q: *What do you think? Does it mean that Jack should stop doing these things?*

We must be clear in understanding that **repentance does not mean that we stop doing things that we enjoy**.

It means we stop doing things that are sinful and anger God. **Having a pint with our mates is not sinful. <u>Getting drunk with our mates is</u>**. In some cases people who are alcoholics will have to stop drinking altogether to avoid temptation. When we come to believe in Jesus and repent of our sin we are basically declaring war against our old self. Instead of loving our sin and bragging about it we begin to hate it and fight against it.

JACK

But how do you know when somebody has truly repented or if they're just bragging about it?

When someone genuinely repents of their sin, and puts their faith in Christ, the Bible says that they are given new spiritual life. When that happens, **their life changes** — it might not be immediately, or quickly and perhaps not even steadily. But their lives do change; they begin to bear, what the Bible calls, fruit. The Bible says that Christians are to be marked by that same kind of love, compassion, and goodness that Jesus showed. So when people are given new spiritual life, they begin to do the kinds of things that Jesus did, to live like Jesus lived, and to bear this good fruit.

Now this fruit doesn't save us. We don't rely on this fruit for our salvation. The fruit we *bear* is just that — the fruit of a tree already made good by God's grace in Jesus. So on the last day, when we face our Maker, we'll not be able to pull out our church attendance record to impress Him. We won't be able to say what a great dad we were, or mum we were, or son we were. We won't be able to point to our own personal purity. Or to the fact that at least we weren't as bad as our next door neighbour. The only defence, the only plea that will do is Jesus Christ and His righteousness.

JACK

Well, I feel like I am ready to trust in Jesus and repent from my sins. What do I do? Is there something I need to say or do to make it happen?

COUNT THE COST

Jack needs to understand that trusting in Jesus and repenting are easier said than done. Becoming a Christian may turn out to be a costly business. Many people in the world are signing their death warrant when they profess faith in Jesus. Many of the earliest believers in the Bible suffered greatly for their new faith.

So, before Jack makes any sort of commitment to Jesus he needs to count the cost. Is he willing to walk away from family and friends who may lead him into sin? Is he willing to delete his drug supplier's name from his cell phone? Is he willing to delete his social media if that is how he makes appointments with various girls? Is he willing to be in it for the long haul when the going gets tough?

Living the Christian life is not an easy thing.

When we make a promise to God we should not do it lightly.

If we want to repent and believe, it won't be an easy life but it will be the best life.

JACK
I understand. I still want to repent and believe. What do I do?

Simply this.

Stop the life you are living right now and commit to turning from it and toward Jesus. Literally, turn your back on your sin and confess your need of Jesus. Ask God to save you and ask Him to help you to live this new life with Him at the centre.

Put your faith in Jesus alone.

Believe in Jesus and the work He finished on the cross. Believe that there is nothing you can say or do to please God.

CHAPTER 8

Rest in Christ and His work on the cross.

Find a good church that will love you, accept you and help you to learn more about God from the Bible.

The church is so important in the life of the Christian. It is there we will find other Christians who will help us in our new life.

Find a church that follows the teachings of the Bible.
Find a church that teaches we are saved only through faith in Jesus.
Find a church that will help you to study the Bible regularly.

Finally, share the good news about what Jesus has done for you.

Tell your family.

Tell your friends.

After all, if you don't, then who will?

SUMMARY

It all seems so simple and yet impossibly difficult to Jack. For the first time in his life he believes that the Bible is true, that God is real, that he is a sinner and guilty before a Holy God, and that Jesus is the Son of God, sinless in every way, who came to earth to be killed for the forgiveness of sins. Jack is amazed by the love of God. He is overcome with a sense of grief about his own sin. It is as if his eyes had been opened and he begins to see for the first time. After hearing this good news about Jesus, Jack decides to pray to God in order to ask God to forgive him of his sin and to declare to God that he has repented and put his faith in Jesus.

JACK

Little does he know that his battles are only just beginning. A spiritual war is coming...

Also available
from
Christian Focus Publications

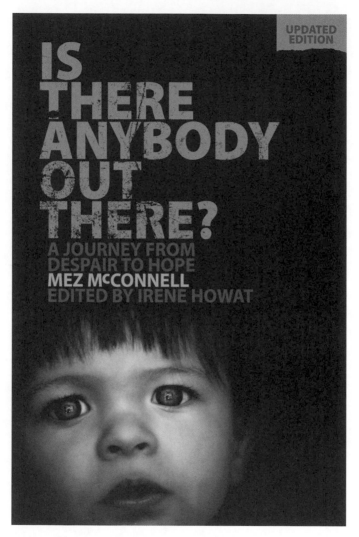

UPDATED
EDITION

IS
THERE
ANYBODY
OUT
THERE?
A JOURNEY FROM
DESPAIR TO HOPE
MEZ McCONNELL
EDITED BY IRENE HOWAT

ISBN 978-1-84550-773-2

What's the Point of Life?
MEZ McCONNELL

Since the publication of 'A child called "it"' by Dave Pelzer there hasn't been a story like this. But this is not just another harrowing story about an excruciating childhood and the ravages on a life it produces. The difference is that Mez not only escaped from his 'trial by parent' but he discovered a hope that has transformed his life. He in turn has helped others find hope in their lives. Mez's story is told with a frankness and wit that hides much of the pain and despair that was his everyday experience. Do you like happy endings? Mez still suffers from his experiences but you'll be amazed at how far you can be restored from such a beginning.

This is a compelling, gripping, heart-wrenching, you-can't-put-it-down story of sin and grace. Read this and thank God that, as Psalm 136 says, 'His love endures forever.'

Mark Dever
Senior Pastor, Capitol Hill Baptist Church and President, 9Marks.org,
Washington, DC

It's an amazing, arresting and touching story.

J. I. Packer
Well known Author & Board of Governors' Professor of Theology,
Regent College, Vancouver, Canada

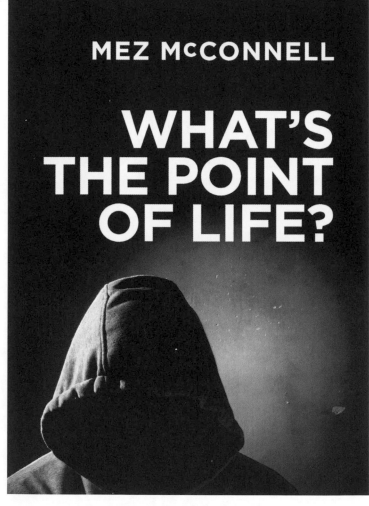

MEZ McCONNELL

WHAT'S THE POINT OF LIFE?

ISBN 978-1-78191-355-0

What's the Point of Life?
Mez McConnell

'Abandoned by my mother, I was often clueless about my father's whereabouts, while his girlfriend – a cruel, angry, and violent woman "looked after us". She wasn't nice and would get angry with us kids and hit us. She would get angry a lot.'

You might think that this is just another harrowing story about an excruciating childhood but the difference is that Mez discovered a hope that transformed his life.

It's an amazing story that shows God's love for sinners and reminds us that no one- no matter who they are or what they've done- is beyond His reach.

Free
Youth Magazine Free Church of Scotland

MAGNIFICENT OBSESSION
WHY JESUS *IS* GREAT
DAVID ROBERTSON

ISBN 978-1-78191-271-3

Magnificent Obsession
Why Jesus *is* Great
DAVID ROBERTSON

David Robertson, author of *The Dawkins Letters*, was told by the leader of an atheist society: 'Okay, I admit that you have destroyed my atheism, but what do you believe?' His answer was 'I believe in and because of Jesus.' This book shows us why Jesus is the reason to believe. In response to the shout of 'God is not Great' by the late Christopher Hitchens, David shows us why Jesus *is* God and *is* Great.

I love this book! It's an excellent, conversational introduction to Christianity for non-Christians and new Christians who are wrestling with questions.

Jon Bloom,
President, Desiring God, Minneapolis, Minnesota

Engaging and insightful... This book is useful no matter what your experience and where you stand on matters of faith.

Tim Keller
Senior Pastor, Redeemer Presbyterian Church, New York City, New York

David Robertson, author of *The Dawkins Letters* and *Awakening*, is pastor of St Peter's Free Church of Scotland in Dundee. Robertson is a trustee of the Solas Centre for Public Christianity and works to fulfil the Centre's mission to engage culture with the message of Christ.

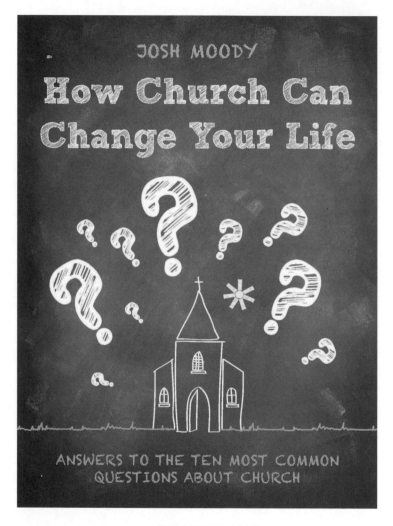

JOSH MOODY

How Church Can Change Your Life

ANSWERS TO THE TEN MOST COMMON
QUESTIONS ABOUT CHURCH

ISBN 978-1-78191-611-7

How Church Can Change Your Life

Answers to the Ten Most Common Questions About Church

JOSH MOODY

Google books on church, there will be no shortage of choice! Some will be helpful, others less so. So why another book on church? Josh Moody, is, in fact, asking a very different question: why should I go to church at all? Filled with practical advice, this book will help you answer questions you maybe should have known the answer to and other questions you never knew to ask!

.. a powerful and needed reminder of the central role the local church should play in the life of every Christian.

R. Albert Mohler
President, The Southern Baptist Theological Seminary, Louisville, Kentucky

This book answers questions about the church that your friends are asking!... Read this book and be encouraged by his answers, and then pass it along to a friend who has considered church attendance to be optional.

Erwin Lutzer
Senior Pastor, Moody Church, Chicago, Illinois

Josh Moody is Senior Pastor of College Church in Wheaton, Illinois. His books include *Burning Hearts, Journey to Joy, No Other Gospel,* and *The God-Centered Life.* For more, visit www.GodCenteredLife.org.

IX 9Marks Urban

For many, areas of poverty are no-go areas; for others, they are simply a place to call home.

Your community needs healthy churches to be a display of God's glory faithfully preaching the gospel and making disciples. No matter where in the world you might be, that is our universal need. This is no less true in our poorest communities. Simply put, building healthy churches is a ministry of mercy and compassion.

What does a healthy church look like in the barrios of Mexico City or the slums of Mumbai? How do we do discipleship and discipline in Scotland's schemes or Atlanta's west end? How do we reach the immigrant or counsel the victim of abuse? How do we train leaders indigenous to poor communities?

9Marks Urban is a 9Marks Initiative to help church leaders think through these questions and more. We produce resources, host events and provide training to equip leaders to build healthy churches in poor communities.

9Marks Urban brings together church leaders from the world's poor communities in order to share their insights and experiences. Visit www.9marks.com for regular articles from these leaders, videos of their conversations, and opportunities to join us at 9Marks Urban events.

Christian Focus Publications

Our mission statement –

STAYING FAITHFUL

In dependence upon God we seek to impact the world through literature faithful to His infallible Word, the Bible. Our aim is to ensure that the Lord Jesus Christ is presented as the only hope to obtain forgiveness of sin, live a useful life and look forward to heaven with Him.

Our books are published in four imprints:

CHRISTIAN FOCUS

Popular works including biographies, commentaries, basic doctrine and Christian living.

CHRISTIAN HERITAGE

Books representing some of the best material from the rich heritage of the church.

MENTOR

Books written at a level suitable for Bible College and seminary students, pastors, and other serious readers. The imprint includes commentaries, doctrinal studies, examination of current issues and church history.

CF4•K

Children's books for quality Bible teaching and for all age groups: Sunday school curriculum, puzzle and activity books; personal and family devotional titles, biographies and inspirational stories – because you are never too young to know Jesus!

Christian Focus Publications Ltd,
Geanies House, Fearn, Ross-shire,
IV20 1TW, Scotland, United Kingdom.
www.christianfocus.com
blog.christianfocus.com